Giovanna Magi

HOLLAND

118 Photographs in colour

BONECHI

© Copyright 1978 by CASA EDITRICE BONECHI
Via dei Cairoli 18b – 50131 Firenze
Telex 58323 CEB

Photographs by Ronald Glaudemans and by: VVV, Den Haag,
pages 6, 47, 53 (above right); Articapress, Haarlem, pages 35;
Slagboom Luchtfotografie, Middelburg, pag. 88.

Translated by: Merry Orling

ISBN 88-7009-046-9

A BRIEF HISTORICAL OUTLINE

When the Romans reached the mouth of the Rhine River in the year 50 B.C., they found themselves in a flat, sandy region, chilled by the cold north winds and prone to frequent flooding by the North Sea. They also found several tribes, perhaps of Germanic origin, who lived by hunting and fishing. The central region was occupied by the Batavians, as mentioned by Plinius, while the Franks, a Celtic race, had settled in the south, and the Frisians thrived in the north. The Saxons, the most Germanic of all, lived mainly in the region northeast of the Rhine. Nevertheless, despite their common origin, these populations differed greatly from one another. At first, it seemed that the Roman conquest was a boon to all, but soon revolts broke out; the first to rebel were the Frisians, followed by the Batavians. Both tribes joined together in 68-70 A.D. under the leadership of Claudius Julius Civilis, who was the organizer of the whole revolt. Nevertheless, the Romans were able to keep their legions in the territory for over three centuries — it was not until 300 A.D. that the pressure of the Germanic tribes began to make headway against the Roman domination. The Batavians were wiped out almost immediately and only the Frisians in the north managed to survive and oppose the Frankish onslaught. It was just as hard to Christianize the region as it had been to conquer it. In the south the conversion of the heathen was carried on by the Merovingian kings, in the north by two Anglo-Saxon missionaries, St. Willibrord and St. Boniface. Yet, the Frisians, for example, stubbornly clung to their paganism for at least two hundred years. During the Carolingian domination the emphasis on evangelization continued. On one hand, Charlemagne used force to subdue the Frisians and Saxons, while on the other, he gave them the laws that would govern them for centuries. At the same time, he divided the country into various provinces ruled by counts, who were actually vassals of the emperor. But even at this time the Dutch not only had to wage war against the elements, the most terrible of which was the sea, but they also had to stand up to just as dreadful human foes, the Vikings, whose savage incursions and forays meant the sacking, looting, and devastation of the Dutch towns. In 841 Charlemagne died and his vast Carolingian empire began to fall apart. Several power struggles later, Holland, and with her, Belgium found themselves part of the Germanic empire. During the Middle Ages, the Netherlands existed as a group of regions under the rule of the Counts of Gelder and Holland, the Duke of Brabant, and the Bishop of Utrecht. This period of Dutch history is mainly characterized by the internecine fighting among the various townships, by now wealthy and powerful in their own right, although foreign dynasties, such as those of Wittelsbach, Bohemia, Luxemburg, and Burgundy, would later overcome the local ones. The Burgundy dynasty managed to dominate all the others when Philip the Bold married Margaret of Flanders; his grandson, Philip the Good, went about consolidating his grandfather's power by creating a huge state which took in all the other provinces and setting up a powerful regular army. He established provincial courts (administrative and law), and was also

3

responsible for the creation of the office of stathouder, a kind of governor who officially represented the emperor, wielding both political and military authority. Philip the Good was succeeded by Charles the Bold who died in a battle against the Swiss in the year 1477. Charles was succeeded by his daughter, Marie of Burgundy, who having married Maximilian of Austria, son of the emperor Frederick III, brought the Netherlands under Austrian domination. In 1500, Charles, the son of Isabella of Castile and Ferdinand of Aragon, was born in Gand. He was king of Spain by way of his mother, and Duke of Burgundy and the Netherlands by way of his father. In 1519 upon the death of his grandfather, Maximilian of Austria, he was elected Holy Roman Emperor and at this point he could truly boast that the sun never set on his empire. As comprehensive and tolerant as he was in political matters, Charles V, a devout and zealous Catholic, could not accept the Protestant religion of the Netherlands. It was under his reign — as enlightened as it was in other respects — that the religious persecutions got underway. At the same time, the development of the Reformation and the resulting Dutch opposition to the Catholic religion, had a dual effect, for it was at the same time a fight to uphold a principle and a way of opposing the foreign invaders. In 1555, following Charles V's abdication, Charles' son, Philip, rose to the throne. He was completely unlike his father. Having grown up in Spain, he spoke neither French nor Dutch, and worse still, he had no inkling of what the problems of his subjects were. In short, his way of thinking, cultural background, and character were all thoroughly Spanish. A tremendous unbridgeable gap developed between Philip and the Dutch people who in the meantime had become more and more firmly entrenched in the Calvanist doctrines. This led to the formation of a movement to oppose the heavy-handed Spanish interference into Dutch affairs. The leaders of the anti-Spanish movement were the Count of Egmont, the Count of Hornes, and the Prince of Orange, William of Nassau, called "Willem de Zwijger," that is to say, William the Silent, because he used to keep his mouth shut and his ears wide open. During the months of August-September 1566 the exasperation and rage of the people boiled over. Churches and monasteries were sacked, profaned, burnt, and destroyed. Philip's reaction was swift and terrible. He sent the Duke of Alba, otherwise known as the "Iron Duke" at the head of a mighty army to crush the country under a reign of terror. The result was numerous executions, among which those of the Count of Egmont and the Count of Hornes, the death sentence was inflicted on William of Orange (who in the meantime had fled the country), and the rebel cities were sacked and burned down. This marked the start of a long and bloody war between Spain and the Netherlands, still torn by the fierce internal conflicts between Catholics, Lutherans, and Calvinists then raging. The outcome of this bitter struggle was the Union of Utrecht of 1579 which established the full autonomy of the Seven Provinces of the North and designated Dutch as the official language of the country. In 1584, in Delft, a Frenchman named Balthazar Gérard assassinated William the Silent and the leadership of the opposition passed to his son Maurice — who repeatedly offered the Dutch crown to Henry III of France and Elizabeth of England, trying to exploit their fierce rivalry with Spain. Things took a turn for the better when the Dutch made up their minds to rely on themselves and on themselves alone; thus the Republic of the United Provinces with the States General at the head of it was born from the ashes of the Union of Utrecht. Under the command of Prince Maurice the united army aided by the British fleet was able to defeat the Spaniards on both sea and land, so that in 1609 Philip was forced to acknowledge the independence of the Dutch republic and sign a twelve year truce with its representatives. Under the Treaty of Westphalia signed in 1648, all of the European powers recognized the new state, although this did much to increase the hostility of the great naval powers, mainly England. Thus Holland, her independent status no longer threatened, could concentrate her efforts on economic development, the result of which was that shortly afterwards, she became the richest state in Europe. Dutch ships sailed the high seas in direct competition with the British fleet and when Spain refused access to the Portuguese ports, the Dutch went off to Java to load their cargos of precious spices. Then, in 1602 Johan von Oldenbarnevelt founded the East India Company, soon followed by the West India Company in 1621. From faroff Oriental and African trade routes, Holland's merchant ships brought home spices, salt, gold, rice, ivory, and perfumes. The Dutch who stayed home were kept busy too — they were engaged in weaving, shipbuilding, herring fishing, whale hunting, diamond cutting, and ceramic making. Merchants and the middle class in general came to dominate the whole structure of Dutch society. The economic boom was paralleled by a cultural flowering, especially in the fields of art and philosophic thought. Little Holland gave the world geniuses such as Erasmus, Spinoza, Grotius, Rembrandt, Frans Hals, and Hobbema. The exciting intellectual atmosphere and the stimulating liberty in the intellectual world even attracted a great thinker like Descartes who spent 20 years of his life in Holland and wrote his Discourse on Method in Leyden. Great spiritual discoveries went hand in hand with great geographical discoveries: Tasmania, New Zealand, the Cape of Good Hope, and Cape Horn were discovered and explored. A group of Dutch pilgrims settled in the colony of New Amsterdam, later known as New York. All of this wealth and splendor began to excite the jealousy of England, Holland's biggest rival on the seas. After numerous skirmishes, Cromwell got the English Parliament to approve the Navigation Act in 1651. It provided that foreign ships could only unload goods from their own territories in English ports and in addition were obliged to render homage to Britain's naval power. In short, the English demanded that their supremacy be recognized. The constant battles they were compelled to wage against the British wore down the Dutch people's resistance and self-confidence. A number of their colonies were lost and several ports could no longer be considered safe. After England, it was France's turn to undermine the shaky Dutch empire.

A polder being dried out.

Louis XIV, in keeping with his expansionist aims, managed to mobilize several anti-Dutch powers, thereby forcing the Netherlands to take part in several exhausting joint wars. It was not until 1697 and the Peace Treaty of Ryswick that the long struggle finally drew to an end. At that point, the current Stathouder of Holland, William III of Orange, as husband of Mary, daughter of James II, was already king of England and could justly rejoice in the diplomatic victory he had been able to procure, i.e. the Netherlands, England, Prussia, and Austria were allied together in a joint effort against the Catholic countries, France and Spain. When William died in 1702, the Orange dynasty died with him and the leadership passed to the Orange-Nassau line (which still rules Holland). Throughout the 18th century there was an alternation of republican and monarchist sentiment, whereby creating fertile terrain for the new ideas filtering in from revolutionary France. The army of the Convention entered the Netherlands, thus putting an end to the existence of the almost 200 year old Republic of the Seven Provinces. The last of the stathouders, William V, crossed the English Channel and sought refuge in England. The state born from this insurrection in 1795 was known as the Batavian Republic, but it was extremely short-lived, for in 1806 Napoleon Bonaparte set his brother Louis upon the Dutch throne. Louis was able to win the affection of his subjects in brief time, but the "continental blockade" brought about the rapid decline of Dutch overseas trade. The Netherlands was thus annexed to the empire and in 1810 became a province of France. In 1813 the dynasty of the Orange was restored, and on November 30 the son of William V, who had taken the name William I, landed in Scheveningen. After the French defeat at Waterloo, the joint forces decided to

A typical view of the tulip fields.

reunite the northern and southern Low Countries in a single realm. The decision was sanctioned by the Congress of Vienna in 1815 and Holland, Belgium, and the Duchy of Luxemburg were united in the Reign of the Low Countries under the rule of William I of Orange-Nassau. This proved to be a terrible mistake, since after more than two hundred years of political, linguistic, religious, and economic separation, the northern and southern provinces were divided by an unbridgeable gap: the northern population was Protestant and spoke Dutch, the southerners Catholic and spoke French, while the Flemish spoke Dutch, but they too were Catholic. These factors were further complicated by the political aspirations of the English who, fearing a strong naval rival on the North Sea, did their best to exploit the rebellious uprisings in Belgium and strongly backed its independence movement. This diplomatic coup reached its goal when in 1831 after a pacific revolution, Belgium broke away from the Low Countries and Leopold of Saxe-Coburg, grandson of the English king George IV, rose to the throne. Under the next two monarchs, William II and

William III, Holland enjoyed a long stretch of relative economic well-being and renewed expansion. Agriculture, industry, and commerce once more flourished, Indonesia was colonized, and social reforms could be enacted. The neutrality proclaimed by Holland in World War I did much to further her political prestige. William III's reign was of brief duration and his daughter Wilhelmina soon succeeded him. Then, during the night between May 9 and May 10, 1940, despite the country's declared neutrality, Hitler's troops overran the Dutch borders and started bombing the country. No previous warning and no formal declaration of war had been issued. This shameful event was followed by five long years of blood and tears for the Dutch people who were encouraged to resist bravely by their Queen from her London exile. Finally, in 1945 the country was liberated. In 1948, after a reign which had spanned almost 50 years, Wilhelmina abdicated in favor of her daughter Juliana who, starting from the post-war period and continuing up to our day, has been witness to Holland's rebirth and renewed splendor.

THE HAGUE

The Hague has a different name in practically every tongue, but its official name is actually 's Gravenhage which the Dutch prefer to abbreviate as Den Haag. The city is first mentioned in a document dated 1242 as "Die Haghe," or the hunting reserve of the Counts, as the counts of Holland originally had a hunting lodge in the woods which once covered the present site of the city. This early construction was thereafter transformed into a castle by William II of Holland who, once he was crowned Emperor of the Roman-Germanic Empire in 1247, was anxious to possess a residence worthy of his new title. The castle was enlarged under his son, Count Floris V and, along with the royal residence, the settlement which had meanwhile sprung up around it, started to expand. This development continued right into the 14th century when Albert of Baveria, regent of Holland, set up his court there and the castle became the official residence of the Stathouder while the new city became the seat of the central government. In 1586 the meeting of the General States of the Netherlands, then in revolt against the Spanish dominion, was held here, but oddly enough, despite these illustrious precedents, it was not until Louis Bonaparte was made king of Holland by his brother Napoleon I, that The Hague

The Vijver.

The Binnenhof with
the Ridderzaal Building.

Mauritshuis: the room with the Anatomy Lesson by Rembrandt.

The interior of the Ridderzaal.

was fully acknowledged as a major city (though the king had originally taken up residence in Utrecht and later moved to Amsterdam). When the house of Orange rose to the throne, The Hague resumed its diplomatic importance and became a kind of headquarters for international conferences: in 1899, 1907, 1929, and 1930 important ones were held here. Still the seat of numerous international organizations, the territory of The Hague, now joined up with the suburbs of Scheveningen, reaches the coast. This is another factor which adds to the quaint charm of this city, modern in some ways, antique and aristocratic in others; it is also a garden city

thanks to the number and size of the public and private parks which dot its territory. Sightseeing in The Hague is a truly unforgettable experience. The city is crammed with historical monuments, picturesque streets and corners to discover unexpectedly, as well as striking oddities. The great architectural complex of the old residence of the Stathouder is today a series of buildings and squares which serve to esthetically enliven the city center. The Binnenhof (literally, inner court) is wholly dominated by the façade of the Ridderzaal, or Knights' Hall, one of the loveliest works of Gothic civic architecture in the city. The building, e-

9

The Gevangepoort.

The Oude Stadhuis. ▶

rected by Floris V in 1280, presents a majestic triangular-shaped façade flanked by cylindrical towers. The inside consists of a single hall covered by a wooden beam ceiling. Here every year on the third Tuesday of September, called Prinsesdag, the Queen solemnly opens the new session of Parliament by reading the Crown's statement to the nation. She arrives at the Ridderzaal in a gilded coach drawn by 8 horses with an escort made up of members of the various branches of the armed forces, "gromms," and soldiers clad in the livery of the House of Orange.

The ceremony itself is quite solemn and dignified, but, at the same time, simple and understated. The Dutch appreciate the simplicity of their sovereign, which is one of the reasons for their longstanding affection for the members of the House of Orange. While Binnenhof means

The Groote Kerk.

The Royal Palace with the statue of William the Silent.

inner court, Buitenhof means outer court. This huge bustling square, now the much trafficked center of the downtown area, was originally the outer courtyard belonging to the Binnenhof. Today it provides everything that the sightseer could ever desire: department stores, banks, and famous typically Dutch eating spots. Nearby is the Gevangepoort, an old city gate to the Binnenhof. Originally built out of wood in the 13th century and later rebuilt as a prison, the building now houses a small museum of torture instruments with several exhibits of the devices used for that purpose in bygone days. It was here that Cornelis de Witt, wrongfully charg-

ed with having participated in the conspiracy which led to the assassination of the Prince of Orange, was imprisoned. When de Witt's brother, the great statesman and then Prime Minister, Jan de Witt came to the prison so that he could intercede on his brother's behalf, the citizenry, boiling with anger and hate, rose up and brutally massacred the two brothers. Today a statue of Jan de Witt proudly looks down at the Plaats, a huge square, once filled with old houses which were torn down to make way for the elegant boutiques now surrounding it. The pride of the city, and one of its best-known features, is the Vijver, the waterway in which many

of the most beautiful monuments of the city are reflected. The most important is the Mauritshuis, a graceful Renaissance palace which, despite its small size, contains one of the world's greatest art collections. The building was commissioned by General John Maurice of Nassau, governor of Brazil. Designed by Jacob van Campen, it was constructed by Pieter Post between 1633 and 1644. Van Campen's design, combining the harmonious proportions of a two storey plan and the simplicity of the Italian style, is a outstanding example of pure elegance and sobriety. The collection of paintings hanging within goes back to the personal

13

collections once belonging to the Dutch Stathouder and the House of Orange. The small number of rooms contains a large number of masterpieces: some of the finest works of Rembrandt (the Anatomy Lesson, a portrait of Homer, and four self-portraits), Vermeer (View of Delft), and Jan Steen (Lady Eating Oysters) are displayed in the ten-odd rooms in which the golden age of Dutch painting is vividly brought to life. Looking at the building, we realize how much simplicity is part of the Dutch character, be it in the public or private sphere. In short, it is striking to see a royal palace which has hardly anything royal about it. The old Koninklijk Paleis, built in 1533 and restored in 1640 by Pieter Post and van Campen stands practically spartan in its linearity before the equestrian statue of William the Silent by the Nieuwe Kerk, erected in 1845. Today the building houses an institute of Social Studies and the Queen has chosen to take up residence in the quiet of her country palace in Soestdijk, not far from Hilversum. Quite the opposite effect is made by the imposing Groote Kerk or Sint Jacobskerk, a Protestant church erected in the Gothic style during the mid 1500s. The church boasts the biggest carillon in all of Holland. Another majestic building is the Oude Stadhuis, started in 1565, but remodelled and enlarged in the 1700s. In addition to these older monuments, The Hague also contains several more recent ones; these are mainly to be found in the northern quarters of the city. A noteworthy example is the Plein 1813 which is a vast oval-shaped

The Plein 1813.

The Vredespaleis.

square set amidst estates and parks. In the 19th century the Dutch national monument was erected here. It depicts a personification of Holland surrounded by allegorical figures and statues of Dutch patriots.

Another example is the Vredespaleis, the Palace of Peace, which was inspired by the Flemish architectural style of the Middle Ages, but which was actually built between 1907 and 1913. The building was

an initiative of Czar Nicholas II who was strongly in favor of holding a new world peace conference in 1898 which would once and for all put an end to the wars afflicting humanity.

A room in the Mesdag Museum.

One of the most intriguing figures representing the Dutch Humanistic spirit is Hendrik Willem Mesdag, born in 1831 in Groningen. Son of a banker, he began following his father's footsteps, until, aged 35, he decided to dedicate himself wholly to painting. His decision to change his lifestyle so radically was supported by his wife, S. van Houten, who was also a painter.
Husband and wife left Holland for Brussels where they studied under established artists until they returned to The Hague and Scheven-ingen where Mesdag could put into pratice the teachings of his master, Willem Roëlofs; Roëlofs had opened his eyes to the "en plein air" style which had been championed by the French Barbizon School. While working as a painter — and he even reaped some success when a seascape of his won a prize — he also started collecting paintings, china, and silver. The whole collection put together by the Mesdags, and the house bought especially to show it off, were donated to the state in 1930 with the clause that nothing could ever be added or removed.
The fact that Mesdag's collection is the result of pure personal taste and nothing else makes it truly unique. Even if there are no real masterpieces in it, it still reveals the social and cultural milieu of Mesdag's time. In fact, as representative of the style of his day, he collected Dutch and French naturalistic and pre-impressionist painters, foremost of whom are Millet, Theodore Rousseau, Courbet, and Daubigny.

Madurodam.

One can't exactly call Madurodam a city, even though it certainly has the appearance of one. It has in fact a bit of all the cities in the Dutch realm, including all their special characteristics and features. We are of course referring to the miniature city, Madurodam, built to 1 : 25 scale, which provides a taste of all the Dutch architectural styles, so that after a visit one can practically say he has seen something of every city in Holland. No detail has been neglected. There is a harbor with ships docked and a lighthouse, as well as amusement parks with rides in action and music-making organs; cars drive along the motorways, and the trains punctually stop at every station, while the windmills turn and the cranes in the shipyards dip up and down. Madurodam is especially fascinating at night when everything is lit up and life continues in the liliputian world. Set up in 1952, it was named after a brave Dutch resistance fighter, George Maduro, who met his death in the concentration camp of Dachau in 1940.

17

Scheveningen beach.

SCHEVENINGEN

Scheveningen, actually the outskirts of The Hague, is one of the foremost resort towns of Holland (though we must not fail to mention Katwijk, Noordwikjk, and Zandvoort). In the 14th century it was a little fishing village; then, over 150 years ago, it was transformed into a resort. In the summer months Scheveningen is alive with thousands of tourists, many of whom come from across the West German border. The Kurhaus (opened in 1885) is the most important establishment in town. Meeting place of the cream of the European nobility at the turn of the century, it is the major drawing card of the town. In 1961 a tremendous pier stretching 400 meters into the water was put up. It has three round buildings which contain a solarium, a restaurant, and a 46 meter tall observation tower. The beach is protected from the violent high tides of the North Sea by stone jetties placed in the water.

DELFT

The city of Delft is renowned for its charming canals and the quaint old houses reflected in them, but mention of its name immediately conjures up the unique blue and white china the city is so famous for — so much so that it has been dubbed the Faenza of Holland. The art of ceramic-making in Delft goes back many centuries: in the 17th century at least 30 factories were known to be in existence. This art however had reached Holland much earlier when a group of Italian craftsmen settled in Holland at the beginning of the 16th century and opened up ceramic tile workshops. As soon as their businesses started to prosper, they took on Dutch names and founded schools to perpetuate their craft. Wall tiles and quaint ceramic stoves as well as tableware and decorative pieces were adorned with the famous Delft blue coloring. The period of greatest splendor was reached in the 18th century, although in the late 1700s, when printed English porcelain had started competing with the hand painted Delft china, numerous factories were forced to close down. Then in 1876 two enterprising businessmen revived the declining china industry by setting up a factory (thereafter known as the Royal Delft Chinaworks) on a mass production basis.

Delft is also the birthplace of two great men: Hugo de Groote (or Hugo Grotius) who was well-known as a jurist, diplomat, philosopher, and poet, and Jan Vermeer whose paintings perfectly reflect the city's peaceful charm. The center of the city is the marketplace, known as the Markt, which also serves as a a delightful setting for summer carillon concerts. On this square rises the Nieuwe Kerk, a Protestant church originally built of wood, but later rebuilt in stone between 1384 and 1496. Alongside the church

The Nieuwe Kerk. ▶

The interior of the Nieuwe Kerk with William the Silent's tomb in the background. ▶

The Huis Lambert van Meerten Museum of Ceramics.

stands a lovely Gothic belltower. 109 meters tall; the tower is rectangular at the base and octagonal at the top. The aisles of the church and the well-lit nave, set off by round columns, have wooden vaulting. Inside is the tomb of the father of the Dutch nation, William of Orange, known as the Silent, who was the first stathouder of the United Provinces of the Netherlands in the 16th century and leader in the struggle against Spanish domination. He was killed on July 10, 1584 by an assassin in the pay of the Duke of Alba. The monument, carved in Italian marble and Dinant stone, was executed by Hendrick de Keyser. At the feet of the reclining effigy figure is a sculpture of the prince's faithful dog who let himself starve to death when his master died. Beneath the sarcophagus is an opening leading to the crypt which contains the remains of forty-odd members of the Orange-Nassau dynasty.

ROTTERDAM

Rotterdam is the second largest city in Holland and since 1968 holds the record as the world's largest port. This gives an idea of the city's incredible development from a settlement on the bank of the tiny Rotte River (which empties into the Maas). A dike on the Rotte is recorded for the first time in a document dated 1283. In 1340 it was granted municiapl rights and ten years later its inhabitants received from the Counts of Holland the authorization to build a canal leading to Leyden and Delft which allowed them to exploit the fast-growing and lucrative commerce of English woolens. This marked the beginning of Rotterdam's growth as a commercial port. Even though the tragic effects of wars and natural disasters at times interrupted the city's economic growth (for example, the siege conducted by Maximilian of Austria in 1489, the fire of 1563, and the sacking and looting by the Spaniards in 1572), the city never ceased its bustling trade, especially with the French ports on the English Channel and the Mediterranean Sea to which it exported its fishing and agricultural products and from which it imported salt, wine, and fruit. The traffic became so heavy that after 1600 Rotterdam was compelled to build a bigger port with ten more especially wide wharves. After 1870 a new waterway, the Nieuwe Waterweg, an eighteen kilometer long, man-made canal was built; it provided faster, more direct access to the sea. This is the period when Rotterdam became a great international port and from then on its traffic has never stopped increasing. The growth was so rapid that between 1870 and 1940 twenty new wharves, some of them gigantic, were built and 117 acres of polder were sacrificed so that Waalhaven, the largest man-made port in the

The Stadhuis.

The Wounded City by Ossip Zadkine.

Erasmus by Hendrick de Keyser.

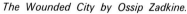

The Euromast. ▶

world, could be constructed. Along with sea trade, numerous related industries, such as oil refineries, shipyards, and the like, sprang up around the port. Unfortunately, Rotterdam suffered terrible damage in World War II. It was in fact the hardest hit of the Dutch cities, mainly on account of the crucial economical and strategical importance it had come to hold. On May 14, 1940 a German air attack sparked a fire which caused the destruction of the whole inner city and a large part of the surrounding area. 25,000 homes, 24 churches, 5000 hotels and restaurants, the city's major monuments such as the Synagogue, the Scottish church, and the headquarters of the East India Com-

pany were among the buildings lost. Later, 125 air raids conducted by the allies who were trying to flush out the Germans still in hiding brought new destruction to the wartorn city. In September of 1944 the German command, fearful of a renewed allied attack, decided to blow up 7 kilometers of dock, whereby rendering the port just about unserviceable. The reconstruction of Rotterdam appeared to be a practically impossible task to everyone but the Dutch. They decided that instead of attempting to reconstruct the old city just as it had been before the war it would be much wiser to build a more modern and efficient one in its place. Later, in commemoration of those

fearless days, a sculpture by Ossip Zadkine called the "Wounded City" was set up in one of the worst ravaged areas. It has come to symbolize the city's rebirth from the ashes of its destruction. Today, the port of Rotterdam which provides dockage for over 30,000 ships yearly, covers a territory of over 30 kilometers in the downtown area of the city, along the banks of the Maas River, and along the Nieuwe Waterweg, the 1870 canal that did so much to spark the city's incredible growth. At the sea end, a huge platform, known as Europoort, has been erected in open sea so that ships too large to reach the city center may be docked. Of course, much of Rotterdam life is closely

associated with the sea. Ample proof is afforded by the famous Maritiem Museum Prins Hendrik which contains over 650 ship models, as well as over 2000 ship designs, nautical maps, atlases, and related documents. But there is another side of the city: it must not be forgotten that Rotterdam is also a center of art and culture. The famous Humanist scholar Geert Geertsz., better known as Erasmus, was born here. A statue of the great thinker rapt in thought, sculpted by Hendrick de Keyser in 1622, has been placed at the corner of Blaak and Coolsingel, the great boulevard which crosses the heart of the city. On the Coolsingel are the most evident signs of the reconstruction of Rotterdam: buildings by Marcel Breuer, a statue by Naum Gabo, and the whole neighborhoods of Bakema and van den Broek. Here on the Coolsingel majestically rises the Stadhuis, the largest town hall in the Netherlands, built between 1914-1920 after the Flemish Renaissance style. But perhaps the loveliest view of this city, so often destroyed and stubbornly reborn each time, may be enjoyed atop the Euromast, the 104 meter tall tower which was put up in 1960 to symbolize Rotterdam's invincible link to the rest of the world as the word "mast" has the same meaning in thirteen different languages.

A bird's eye view is the best way to take in the new city designed and rebuilt according to the most advanced townplanning techniques. Right by the modern and rational center is the old city, characterized by people of every race and color. Rotterdam, more than any other Dutch city, is a successful melting pot of Europeans, Africans, and Asians who live side by side in perfect harmony and accord.

The Westersingel.

A room in the Maritiem Museum Prins Hendrick.

View of the port of Rotterdam.

GOUDA

Gouda acquired municipal rights in the 13th century under the reign of Count Floris V (who met his death in 1296 at the hands of his own nobles). Today the city's chief fame rests on its world famous orange-colored cheese and unusual clay pipes. The Gouda cheeses, weighing up to 40 kilos apiece, are sold in a market held every Thursday morning. Unlike the Alkmaar market where the cheeses are transported by special cheese porters, the Gouda cheeses are stacked high in brightly colored farm wagons. As for the other typical Gouda product, the clay pipe, there is a special museum in the city called the De Moriaan Museum filled with exhibits of the long white pipes we are accustomed to seeing in Dutch paintings. One of the numerous factories which manufactures these pipes, the Goedewaagen Company, is famous for their intriguing "mystery pipes." Brand-new, they are pure white, but they darken with use until a design, unknown to the buyer at the moment of purchase, appears on the bowl of the pipe.

Gouda also has two splendid architectural monuments: the Stadhuis (Town Hall) and the Church of Sint Janskerk (St. John's). The Stadhuis was built between 1447 and 1450 in the High Gothic style. Every half hour its colorful carillon comes to life with figures which illustrate the conferral of municipal rights upon Gouda. The church of St. John was erected later, in 1485, in the late Gothic style, but was rebuilt as a basilica after a fire destroyed it in 1652.

The church is aglow with 70 celebrated Gothic stained glass windows, the masterpiece of the two brothers, Dirk and Wouter Crabeth, who crafted them. The windows were carried out in two campaigns; when the church was still consecrated to the Catholic cult and then after the Reformation had taken place. The earliest group, comprising twelve in all, dates back to 1555-1573. In the 25th window showing the liberation of the city of Leyden, there is a portrait of William the Silent who donated window number 22 to the cathedral. His long-standing rival, Philip II of Spain, not to be outdone, thus donated not one, but two. He is depicted together with his wife, Mary Tudor, in the window portraying the Last Supper.

The Stadhuis.

The interior of the Janskerk.

One of the stained glass windows.

OUDEWATER

Oudewater is one of the oldest cities in Holland. It is also the birthplace of the painter Gerard David and the theologian Arminius, founder of the Jacobite sect. The city, twice destroyed by fire (the second one broke out in 1575), still possesses a number of lovely Dutch Renaissance buildings designed in keeping with the strictest canons of the Renaissance style. The Town Hall with storks picturesquely roosting on the rooftop and the house where Arminius was born are two outstanding examples. But Oudewater's fame rests largely on the presence of a curiousity, i.e. the "heksenwaag," or witches' scale, displayed inside the Waag. This relic, one of a kind, dates back to the long ago period when the city was in the throes of fierce witch hunts. The woman accused of being a witch was brought here and. dressed in a paper gown with a paper broomstick in her hand, was set on the huge scale (incidentally, it was of hairsplitting accuracy) and weighed in presence of the mayor, a city council member, the weights master, and the local midwife. If the weight proved normal, the alleged witch was immediately cleared of the charge since it was evident that a real witch would be balanced upon the broomstick. The woman was also presented with a document certifying that she did not belong to the witches' guild — given the times, this piece of paper was of great value. A certificate is presented to all the tourists willing to get up on the scale for a weighing in.

The witches' scale,

The Stadhuis.

Arminius' house.

SCHOONHOVEN

The town, stituated at the confluence of the Lek and the Vlist Rivers, contains a number of old picturesque buildings, such as the Town Hall, dating from 1452. The bells of the Town Hall were forged by melting down a bronze cannon originally from a ship. In front of the building there is a circle of stones marking the exact spot where an alleged witch was burned at the stake. The church, originally built in the 14th century Gothic style, was later redone in the 1600s. The Het Edelambachtshuis, or goldsmiths' house, has been transformed into a silver and ceramics museum. Here daily shows are put on, during which silversmiths, using old-time tools and techniques, give demonstrations of their craft. The Waag (public weighing station) is another worthwhile sight.

The Stadhuis.

A city gate.

LEYDEN

Leyden may be defined as the most intellectual city of the realm, not only because of its celebrated university, but also for its group of philosophers and scientists who rapidly brought the university to a high European standard. The city grew up along the main branch of the Rhine River: recent excavations have established that by 800 a settlement already existed on the spot. Its Roman name was Lugdunum Batavorum. Shortly after the year 800, the Danish king Harold erected a keep here which would be taken over, a hundred years later, by the Counts of Holland. Under the reign of the Counts, the city, then known as Leithen, expanded and took up trade and commerce, so that by the beginning of the 13th century, it was granted municipal rights. Leyden has become a part of Dutch legend for a memorable historical event. From October 31, 1573 it was besieged by General Valdez, commander of the Spanish troops, who was hoping to conquer the city by starving it into surrender, but after a year had gone by, Leyden was still valorously resisting. The local paupers and beggars, called "gueux," thought up the idea of bringing aid and reinforcement to the besieged city by opening a dike every night, and thus allowing the Dutch fleet, which travelled from one lake to another, to reach Leyden in no time. On October 3, 1574 the siege was lifted and the gueux, thereafter known as "watergeuzen," i.e. water paupers, were able to distribute herring and white bread to the famished city. The episode has become a tradition: on October 3 of every year the Burgomaster distributes the same simple food to the citizens of Leyden so that everyone may remember those formidable days of heroism. Moreover, the history of the university is linked to the very same episode. In order to express his gratitude to the city for the tenacity and courage they had displayed throughout the long siege, William of Orange proposed a choice of one

View of Rapenburg.

or two benefits: either the city could be exempted from paying taxes forever or else be granted its own university. Leyden opted for the latter solution and the following year was endowed with its university campus which from then on became the focal point of the whole town. It was on account of the university that Leyden became the crossroads and meeting place of the intelligentsia of all of Europe. The greatest minds of the 16th and 17th centuries taught in it. We shall briefly mention: the mathematician Snellius, the jurist Hugo de Groot, the physician Boerhave (of whom it was said the address "Boerhave, Europe" was more than enough for the couriers), the botanist Clasius (famous for his experiments on tulips, of which he managed to produce an incredible number of varieties), the physicist Musschenbroek (the inventor of the first condensor), and the physicist Huygens (who set forth the theory of the undulation movement of light), not to mention the philosopher Descartes. During this period Leyden set another record in the field of cultural activity: in 1617 a printing shop specializing in rare languages such as Chinese, Arabic, and Persian was founded. Nevertheless, the city's prosperity was not linked to its cultural fervor, but rather it was based upon an extremely flourishing cloth trade. Whoever loves art will certainly find Leyden a treat. The name of the painter Geerten tot Sint Jans is the first one which comes to mind, immediately followed by Lucas of Leyden. But life was not always easy for Leydon. In 1807 in the center of the attractive neighborhood known as Rapenburg a ship with a cargo of gunpowder exploded and a large section was totally destroyed. This area, for a long time known as the Ruins, has been transformed into the Van der Werf Park. Nevertheless, there

◀ *The Pieterskerk.*

◀ *The Hooglandse Kerk.*

The Bridge of Korensbeursbrug. ▶

The Archeological Museum: the Egyptian Hall.

are still monuments which are living proof of the city's glorious past: the 17th century Stadhuis, destroyed in 1929 (only the façade of which designed by Lieven de Key was partially spared), the picturesque Vismarkt, the old fish market, and the quaint Korenbeursbrug, the bridge where wheat prices were negotiated, with its classical style wooden portico that the local inhabitants call "our own Rialto." In addition to these monuments there are the churches: the Pieterskerk, now Protestant, an imposing double aisled Gothic church consecrated in 1121 and the Hoogland-sekerk, just a tiny wooden chapel dedicated to St. Pancratius in the 14th century, and later rebuilt in the Gothic style two hundred years later. In addition to the churches there are the museums, the foremost of which is the Rijksmuseum van Oudheden (National Museum of Antiquities), one of the greatest archeological museums in all of Europe with its prehistoric, Etruscan, Greek, Egyptian, and Roman collections. On the same level is the Rijksmuseum vor Volkenkunde (Ethnographic Museum) which was founded in 1837, thus making it one of the oldest in Europe. The objects on display are masterpieces of art from the various civilizations ranging from the Americas to Africa and the Orient. Especially noteworthy is the Indonesian collection. We must not overlook the Museum voor de Geschiedenis der Natuurwetensschappen, the National Museum of the History of Science, which contains a huge number of historical instruments and documents and the Stedelijk Museum, also known as Lakenhal, located in the cloth merchants' building, with its collections of 15th, 16th, and 17th century Dutch and Flemish art.

HAARLEM

From the chronicles we learn that Haarlem had obtained municipal rights by the 10th century; fortified in the second half of the 12th, it became the residence of the Counts of Holland. The city did not have an easy time of it: in addition to the traditional battle that the local population was compelled to wage against the enemy from without, the sea, Haarlem was also plagued with other disasters within (three fires, one in 1155, another in 1346, and a third in 1351, and wars). Then, during the Protestant revolt of 1572 the city was subjected to a seven month long siege (lasting from December 11, 1572 to July 13, 1573) conducted by the son of the Duke of Alba, Don Frederick. Equally memorable for its duration and its tragic and glorious episodes, the outcome was terrible. Throughout the long 1572 winter the city stood fast, expecting aid from William the Silent, and was in some way able to resist the whole time, despite the unbearable hunger. When the Spaniards assassinated William, destroyed his fleet, and wiped out the armada which was supposed to be bringing help, the citizens of Haarlem were compelled to surrender, though they hoped that an honorable peace could be reached. But this was not to be the case: the Duke of Alba made the city pay for the seven months of siege he had been forced to conduct and the enormous death toll his troops had suffered and ordered that 1800 survivors of Haarlem be cruelly massacred. The city, though, could not be kept down and when in 1577 the army of the States General was garrisoned here, it embarked on a period of great prosperity. In the 17th century the city's splendor was enhanced by the presence of a group of painters who had either been born in or had taken up residence in Haarlem, the best-known of whom were Frans Hals and Jacob van Ruysdael. In 1862 Haarlem proudly inaugurated a museum dedicated to its most famous native son, Frans Hals, which in 1913 was moved to its present location, the Oudemanne-

Aerial view of Haarlem.

The Groote Kerk with the Vleeshall, or Vishal, beside it.

The Amsterdamse Poort. ▶

huis. This old building had originally been erected by Lieven de Key in 1608 as an old age home, and it was where Hals himself had died. In the 17th century too, in 1636 to be exact, the tulip growing industry was born in Haarlem. During April and May, the fields of "bloemenvelden" stretching south of the city afford one of the most incredible spectacles one can ima-

gine. In addition to this marvel of nature, Haarlem also boasts a number of remarkable architectural monuments. The foremost is the Stadhuis, once residence of the Counts of Holland which, despite an erroneous tradition dating it in the 13th century, was erected in the middle of the 16th century and completed by Lieven de Key in the period 1620-1630. The historical

section of Haarlem, the Grote Markt, is dominated by an imposing church, the Grote Kerk, better known as the Cathedral of St. Bavo. It was built in the Brabantine late Gothic style on the site of a smaller building destroyed in a fire in 1328. Inside there is an extraordinary organ with a triple keyboard, 68 registers, and 5000 pipes, built in 1738 by Christiaan

Müller. The organ case decoration was designed by Daniel Marot. Among the people who have played this organ are Mozart, Handel, and Dr. Albert Schweitzer. The Vleeshall (or Vishal) is a charming contrast to the cathedral. The old meat market is housed in a red brick and stone building erected by Lieven de Key between 1602 and 1623 after the Renaissance style. A taste of Haarlem's glorious military past can be had at the Amsterdamse Poort, the imposing remains of the 15th century walls which once encircled the city. Extant today is a sturdy square tower flanked by two smaller octagonal towers, in front of which protrudes a structure with round turrets. One more interesting historical tidbit about this city so rich in history: here in the second half of the 15th century Laurenz Janszoon Coster invented a printing press just about the same time that Gutenberg invented his in Germany.

The Stadhuis.

A room of the Frans Hals Museum.

BREDERODE CASTLE

There are few places in Holland which can equal the charm of the Brederode Castle with its picturesque ruins salvaged from the sand dunes. Founded in the 13th century and rebuilt in the 15th, it was later enlarged in the 1500s. Its name is linked to a noble family, the de Brederodes, many of whom are well-known figures. Francis de Brederode (1465-1490) who died at the age of 25 from wounds inflicted during a battle in which the Dutch were defeated by Maximilian of Austria's troops and Henry de Brederode who in 1566 presented the famous document signed by the Union of Nobles before the regent Margaret of Parma in Brussels, are two of historical note. The castle walls, which were unearthed in 1862 and then expertly restored, may today be admired in all their splendor. Two towers, one of which was a watchtower, the brick fortification walls, and the moat have all been brought back to light.

The castle of Brederode.

SPAARNDAM

Spaarndam commemorates the charming legend of Pieter and the dike. Situated a kilometer and a half northeast of Haarlem, Spaarndam is where in 1960 Princess Irene officiated at the ceremony inaugurating a monument to the courage, selflessness, and dedication Dutch youth have displayed over the centuries. The statue depicts the famous boy who one day while he was out taking a stroll noticed a breach in one of the dikes. He realized that if it got any larger, it would have meant the destruction of the protective wall and thus the destruction of Haarlem itself. Pieter did not hesitate one moment — he stuck his finger into the hole and kept it there all night until help arrived. Unfortunately, in the meantime Pieter had died, but his fearless sacrifice had avoided a catastrophe for his native city.

The monument to Pieter, the courageous boy from Spaarndam.

OPGEDRAGEN AAN ONZE JEUGD ALS EEN
HULDEBLIJK AAN DE KNAAP DIE HET
SYMBOOL WERD VAN DE EEUWIGDURENDE
STRIJD VAN NEDERLAND TEGEN HET WATER
—o—
DEDICATED TO OUR YOUTH TO HONOR THE
BOY WHO SYMBOLIZES THE PERPETUAL
STRUGGLE OF HOLLAND AGAINST THE WATER

The cheese porters.

The Waag. ▶

ALKMAAR

Cited in a chronicle of the year 800 as Almere, Alkmaar was long a stronghold during the defense waged by the Dutch against the Frisian invaders. Then, besieged in 1573 by Don Federico of Toledo (brother of the Duke of Alba), it was the first Dutch city to withstand the assault of the Spanish troops who were forced to break off their siege and retreat. The city is renowned for its cheese market, the most important in Holland, which is held every Friday in the summer months at 10 am before the public weighing station. The building was originally a chapel consecrated to the Holy Spirit (built in 1386 in the Gothic style, it was later rebuilt in 1582). Pieter Cornelis designed the belltower which was erected between 1595 and 1599. On top is a carillon with horsemen figures by Melchior de Haze (1688).

The round cheeses, weighing anywhere from 2 to 6 kilos, are either yellow (for domestic consumption) or red (for export). The cheeses are transported to the marketplace on huge flat-bottomed barges from which they are tossed to the cheese porters waiting nearby with their gondola-shaped wooden barrows. The porters belong to an old guild which has been granted the exclusive privilege of transporting the cheeses. A "father" supervises teams of 28 porters further divided into 4 sub-groups known as "veems." The veems may be distinguished by the blue, red, green, or yellow ribbon on each porter's straw hat. The task of the porters is to load the cheeses upon special planks which hold at least 80 2-kilo cheeses. They then take them over to the public weigh bridge where the quotations are chalked up on special blackboards. The team that totals the most is awarded the title "guild leader group" and holds the title until market day of the following week. At the end of the market day, the porters all go to drink special beer prepared for the occasion which is served up in special pewter mugs handed down from generation to generation for centuries. This is how cheese has been marketed for the last three hundred years in Alkmaar.

Panorama of Texel.

TEXEL

Originally the Island of Texel was a fief that the Counts of Holland annexed in 1183. Extending over 183 square miles (it is about 15 miles long and more than 5 miles wide), it is the largest of the Wadden Islands which form a natural barrier between the sea and the mainland. Today, over 11,000 people live on Texel scattered among the seven villages of the island. They earn their livelihood mainly from fishing and sheep raising. There is a well-known sanctuary in the region known as De Slufter where numerous fresh-water ponds called "muyen" are to be found. Migrant birds of all species stop over in Texel when it is time to lay their eggs. They flock to the northern end of the island known as Eijerland ("egg-land"), and do not move until the eggs have been hatched.

It is not hard to find a local guide willing to show the tourist this paradise from close up (but not too close up, for there is a certain distance beyond which nobody is allowed to get so that the animals will not be disturbed — and this distance must be respected).

Texel is not just an animal heaven, it is also a kind or earthly paradise for human beings. This oasis of peace and quiet may be toured on foot, horseback, or even on bike. The buses are all marked TESO (standing for Texel's Eigen Stoomboot Onderneming), which is the name of a private transportation company belonging to the inhabitants of the island. All the profits are used for the improvement of the island itself.

AFSLUITDIJK

This dike (literally, the closing dike) holds an essential place in the centuries long, highly dramatic struggle Holland has been waging against the sea. Starting from the 17th century, various ways to separate the Zuider Zee from the North Sea were discussed. Actually the earliest plan dates back to 1667, but the ensuing difficulties always seemed too great to be overcome and no action was ever taken. Then after the catastrophic floods of 1916 it was decided to erect a dike which, by uniting the provinces of North Holland to Friesland, would serve a dual purpose: it would prevent floods from devastating land in the vicinity while at the same time new territory could be reclaimed from the terrible North Sea. Designed by Cornelis Lely in 1892, the dike was begun in 1919 and inaugurated on May 28, 1932. 30 kilometers long and 90 meters wide, it stands 7 meters above mean sea level. 23 million cubic meters of sand, 13 million cubic meters of clay filler, and 1 million blocks for paving the slope were required in its construction. At either end of the dike, locks regulate navigation of the Ijsselmeer, the semi-freshwater lake formed by the closing off of the Zuider Zee. Its total depth is 3.5 meters. At the beginning of the dike, which is surmounted by a four-lane motorway, there is a monument to Cornelis Lely, while upon another monument further along there is an inscription which reads, "A living people builds its future."

The highway on top of the dike.

Sailboats engaged in a race.

Skaters in Friesland.

FRIESLAND

Stretching along the banks of the Ijsselmeer and the North Sea, the province of Friesland is one of the richest regions in Holland. It was already mentioned by Homer, Pliny the Elder, and Tacitus as a treacherous place always covered by fog — in fact, in 325 B.C. the Greek Pytheas dubbed it the "Coast of Terror." This gives us some idea of how hard life was for the inhabitants of the province. The never-ending struggle waged against the sea and natural forces evidently tempered the character of this hardy people; around 50 B.C. they were even able to revolt against the Roman troops and drive them back beyond the Rhine.

We hardly know anything about the origin of the Frisians, although it is believed that they originally came from the Scandinavian peninsula (perhaps Sweden) or that they were of Celtic origin. Nevertheless, it is a fact that the language they speak, while practically incomprehensible to most of the Dutch, is quite similar to the English spoken by the inhabitants of Yorkshire — it is even said that the Yorkshire fishermen can understand their Frisian counterparts. Rigorously autonomous throughout Dutch history (and right through the war against Spain in which the rest of the country was passionately involved), the Frisians also differ from the rest of the population with regards to their ethnic characteristics; their light complexions, blond hair, blue eyes, and tall stature make them much more Scan-

dinavian looking than the rest of the population. They also have their own national anthem and their own flag, which is blue and white with red leaves.

The Frisians earn their living primarily from cattlebreeding, raising the famous black and white spotted "Frisian cows." These cows, which an old country tradition calls the "great mothers," are the world's greatest milk producers. The butter made from this milk, along with English butter, is supposedly the best in the world — or so an old Dutch saying goes.

But Friesland is not only renowned for its agricultural produce. The region is in fact a paradise for boat lovers. The whole countryside is dotted with hundreds of little lakes ventilated by seabreezes which, especially on weekends, come alive,

with all kinds of sailboats, canoas, and rowboats.
Besides sailing, the Dutch love skating, which is their national winter sport. The skating champions all compete in an unusual (and exhausting) race, the Elfstedentocht (11-city race), which entails skating over 200 kilometers.

The Martiniskerk.

The University.

GRONINGEN

Capital of the province of the same name, Groningen is the foremost city of North Holland, especially after the announcement that methane gas deposits were recently discovered in the environs.

The city is extremely old: the name Groningen appears for the first time in a bequest made in 1040 by the German Emperor Henry III to the Bishop of Utrecht. Fortified in 1110, its growth was rapid and in 1229 it joined the Hanseatic League. In 1579 it became a member of the Union of Utrecht and fought valiently against the Spanish who occupied it from 1580 to 1594. At the end of the 17th century it was protected by fortifications, later torn down between 1874 and 1878 to make way for public gardens. Groningen's importance was further enhanced by the founding of a university ranking second only to the University of Leyden. Inside the university building is a lovely auditorium with fine stained glass windows by J. Dijkstra and a Senate Hall decorated with the portraits of the professors who taught there. The heart of the city is the market-place, the Grote Markt, on which we find the neo-classical Stadhuis and the Goudkantoor. The latter has been attributed to Garwer Peters, the same architect responsible for the 17th century fortifications. Today the building is occupied by the Ship Museum which contains fascinating ship models, navigation devices, paintings, anchors, etc.

On the northeastern corner of the square originally stood a Romanesque oratory built either in the 11th or 12th century. At the beginning of the 13th century a church dedicated to the protector of the city, St. Martin, was put up in its place. Only the transept is left of the original 13th century church: the choir with its hexagonal plan was built between 1400 and 1425 and subsequent alterations carried out in the 15th century resulted in enlarging the nave. The church's finest feature, however, is its five storey belltower which is Gothic at the base and Renaissance in the upper storeys. The 315 foot tower (just a bit lower than the belltower of the Cathedral of Utrecht) commands a magnificent view of the city.

MEDEMBLIK

Medemblik, one of the oldest settlements in North Holland, is one of the many "dead cities" to be found in the vicinity of the Zuider Zee. It was in fact the capital of the Frisians even before Hoorn and Enkhuizen ever existed, since, according to tradition, it was founded in 334 A.D. Traces of Medemblik's long ago prosperity are still visible in the warehouses, churches, and dwellings which are living proof of that past glory, later followed by a lengthy unbroken period of silent abandon in the 1700s. Reaching Medemblik by way of Enkhuizen, the first building one notes south of the city is the castle of Radboud, named after a Frisian king who lived in the 8th century A.D. This stronghold, typically medieval in appearance, was rebuilt by Count Floris V in 1288. Partially ruined and demolished in the 17th and 18th centuries, it is nevertheless still an imposing sight with its timeworn bricks and slate roof, rising at the entrance to the harbor.

The castle of Radboud.

ENKHUIZEN

Once a port on the Zuider Zee, Enkhuizen today is a flourishing tulip growing center. It reached the height of its glory in the 17th century when it could boast over 40,000 inhabitants and a fishing fleet of over 400 vessels. Herring fishing brought prosperity to the shipowners who, during the early years of the 17th century, were able to get even richer from the lucrative trade they carried on with the East Indies. Then when the port was filled in (at the time the north dike was being built), thus blocking off any outlet to the sea, Enkhuizen started on a slow, but inevitable decline, the end result of which was that the city eventually became a charming city-museum. Museum too is the Peperhuis, or Spice House, once the biggest warehouse belonging to the East India Company. Inside are objects and documents which give an idea of the architecture, furnishings, dress, and everyday articles of the whole surrounding region. Enkhuizen is particularly known for the Zuider Spui, a charming group of fishermen's houses with quaint slanted fronts. Noteworthy are the striking sculpted façade decorations of the Weeshuis (or Orphanage), dated 1616, and the sturdy Drommedaris, a two-part tower built at the entrance to the old port as part of the city fortifications in 1540. The 16th century carillon on top is famous as the most beautiful in all of Holland.

◀ *The Spui.*

◀ *The Orphanage.*

The Drommedaris Tower.

HOORN

The city was called Hoorn after the horn shape of its port. The horn of plenty is in fact the symbol of the city and we find it carved upon the façades of houses and on the crests of palaces, and painted upon the flags of ships. Already mentioned in 14th century manuscripts, Hoorn grew rapidly. It flourished throughout the 15th century, reaching its height of splendor in the 17th century. It was the birthplace of several great men. The explorer Willem Schouten, the first European to sail around the tip of the South American continent (which he named Hoorn after his native town though it is now called Cape Horn); Abel Tasman, who discovered New Zealand and Tasmania; Jan Pieterzoon Coen who founded Batavia (present-day Jakarta) in Java and who was governor of the island from 1618 to 1629; and Bontekoe, another celebrated explorer of the faroff Indies, who lived in the 17th century, are among the best-known. As was the case for numerous other cities on the Zuider Zee, Hoorn's decline began in the 18th century when the supremacy of the Dutch fleet was overshadowed by the English merchant marine on the great international trade routes. But numerous reminders of Hoorn's past splendor such as the Bossuhuizen (Bossu House), at the end of the Grote Oost are still extant. The Bossuhuizen was named after the Spanish Admiral defeated and taken prisoner aboard his own galleon "The Inquisition" on October 11, 1753 in the vicinity of Cape Horn by the fleets of the cities of Hoorn, Edam, Enkhuizen, and Monnikendam.

The highlights of this battle are illustrated in the sculpture and inscriptions decorating the façade of the house with the winds personified by two figures of nude women.

The Waag with the statue of J. P. Coen.

The Bossuhuizen.

Native costumes of Marken.

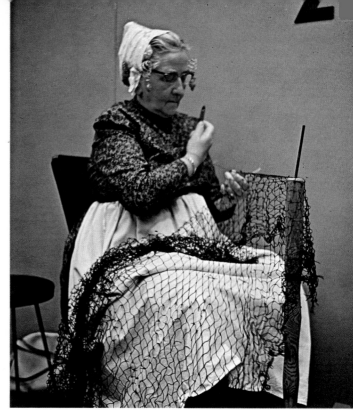

Repairing the nets.
Native costumes of Volendam.

VOLENDAM AND MARKEN

These charming ports have managed to preserve their antique character like few other Dutch cities. Volendam is famous for the handsome native costumes worn by the local inhabitants. These may be admired in the morning hours when the women are on their way to church (the population is mostly Catholic). The women wear pleated blue or black striped jackets over a seven-colored skirt callad a "zvenkleurige rok." Extremely picturesque is their head covering — hiding practically all of the face, it looks like some kind of medieval helmet. The men wear short fitted jackets trimmed with silver buttons, flaring back pants, and round hats. In Marken the little wooden houses painted bright colors and, needless to say, all spotlessly clean, look like ships — their tiny interiors are incredibly but neatly crammed with objects. The inhabitants, mostly Protestants, are mainly fishermen and wear their native dress every day, just as many Dutch people do. The women sport red jackets over colored bodices and wear coifs on their heads. The men wear jackets over loose-fitting trousers, tied at the knee, and black stockings. Both sexes have the typical "klompen," i.e. wooden clogs, on their feet, a charming reminder of the time when Holland was still a primarily agricultural country.

ZAANDAM

The village of Zaandam, renowned for its great shipyards, witnessed a number of historical events. One of the best-known is the visit paid by Peter the Great, Czar of Russia, in 1697. The young monarch was at the time travelling under a false name, Peter Michailov, and working as a common laborer in the shipyards so he could study ship-building techniques. Despite this disguise, his real identity was soon discovered by the local population and he was compelled to flee Zaan-dam and seek refuge in Amsterdam. The home in which Peter lived during his brief stay was donated to Czar Nicholas II who had it restored and turned into a museum. Near the town of Zaan-dam is another noteworthy sight. An entire village has been reconstructed by the banks of the river Zaan. The typical countryside of the North Holland polder has been recreated with the green wooden houses characteristic of this region throughout the 17th and 18th centuries. There is even a restaurant furnished in the old-fashioned Dutch style and of course one can admire different kinds of windmills.

Zaanseschans. ▶

Windmills in Zaandam.

The village along the Zaan. ▶

AMSTERDAM

We have no real information about the foundation of Amsterdam. According to legend, two fishermen, accompanied by their dog, were shipwrecked in a violent storm while on a fishing trip. They set about building a refuge in the swamps where the River Amstel flows into the estuary of the Zuider Zee (also called the Ij) and the settlement founded by the two fishermen and their families who later joined them, is said to be the origin of what we call Amsterdam today. Since the village was located at the mouth of the Amstel River, it was also necessary to construct a dam to protect their homes from the stormy waters. This was the derivation of the city's name, Amstelledamme (dam on the Amstel), which was later changed to Amsterdam. The city is mentioned for the first time by its original name in a charter dated October 27, 1275 in which Floris V granted tax exemption and the right of free trade to its citizens. Amsterdam, which drew its life and livelihood from the water, developed so quickly that by the 17th century it stood out among all the others as queen of the high seas. Diamond cutting and the importation of colonial products such as tea, coffee, tobacco, and cocoa were her major activities. The East and West India companies set up their headquarters in Amsterdam, at which time it was embellished with magnificent mansions along the three huge concentric canals encircling the whole town. Then, Amsterdam's splendor began to wane just about the same time that England and France were on the rise as sea powers. Subjected to Bonaparte's dominion, Amsterdam was the first Dutch city (1813) to rebel against the foreign yoke. She headed the movement which later founded the independent kingdom of Holland. Overrun and occupied by the Nazis in 1940, along with the other Dutch cities, Amsterdam would regain her freedom only five years later.

The Dam, a huge, irregularly-shaped

The Dam.

Begijnhof.

square, is the heart of the city. "Dam" means dike in Dutch and, in fact, it was here that hundreds of years ago Dutch fishermen built their homes so that they would be protected from the perilous waters of the river. Thereafter, the city developed outwards from this point. Even though the square is today mostly filled with modern buildings (some of rather questionable taste), there are also two old buildings of great interest, the Royal Palace, and the Nieuwe Kerk in the center of the photo. The palace, a fine ex-

ample of the Dutch classic style, was built between 1648 and 1655 upon a foundation of 13,659 pylons. The Nieuwe Kerk, of which only the right side is visible, was rebuilt in 1452 after a great fire had destroyed it along with most of the city. The Monument to the Liberation rising in the middle, was built in 1956 by J. Radecker. It was built in memory of the Dutch who perished in World War II. The monument contains 12 urns, each of which is filled with soil from eleven Dutch localities and one with soil from

Indonesia.

There are different versions to account for the origin of the women who dedicate themselves to good works known as Beguines. Some say they were pious women who preferred the cloistered but less rigid life of the Beguinage to the irrevocable vows of the convent. At any rate, once they had entered the institution they dedicated their lives to teaching and caring for the sick. Others say that the Beguines were originally the widows of fishermen who retired to this life,

Oudezijds Voorburgwal n. 19.

Oudezijdas Voorburgwal n. 187.

dedicating themselves to charity and needlework. Whatever the origin of the institution, the Beguinage of Amsterdam (founded in 1346) is one of the finest in the Netherlands. Its courtyard, an oasis of peace in the heart of the city, dates from the 14th century and is surrounded by houses built in the 15th and 16th centuries. Because of alterations and rebuilding over the centuries, the façades and appearance of the houses are often those of the 17th and 18th centuries, but a number of them are much older: the one at No. 34, for example, dates from the 14th century and still has its medieval wooden front intact. After the religious turmoil which followed the Reformation, many of these houses were used as secret Roman Catholic churches.

One of the Beguinage's points of interest is the grave of a Beguine called Cornelia Arens, who asked to be buried in the gutter in order to do penance for the members of her family who had turned Protestant. On May 2 every year there is a picturesque ceremony in which today's Beguines strew her grave with flowers and sand.

Along the Oudezijds Voorburgwal are numerous examples of typical Dutch dwellings. The design of the house at No. 19 *(photo top left)*, built in 1656 as the stone high on the façade says, shows the richest sense of imagination. It has two huge dolphins, the largest in all Amsterdam, on either side of the so-called "neck gable" which crowns the house. The dolphins are linked by huge strings containing countless

shells, yet another example of the life and emblems of the sea which recur in various forms throughout the architecture of Amsterdam. There is another example of a house with a neck gable at No. 187 Oudezijds Voorburgwal *(top right)*. This dwelling, built in 1663 and belonging originally to a merchant, is also called — understandably — the house with the "façade of pillars": the first four pillars are of the Tuscan order, the next four are Ionic and the top two are Corinthian, all being made from brick. At the top are two nude statues of an Indian and a Negro, leaning against a pile of merchandise, including ropes and rolls of tobacco. A scroll in the center hides the arm of the hoist used to lift goods up to the storeroom, the door of which is

58

The Waag or Sint Anthoniespoort.

The Amstel.

The Magere Brug.

below: the storeroom and private residence of the merchant were thus one and the same building. The façade was richly adorned with festoons of fruit, scrolls and ovals. The more sober and simple the lower part of the house was, the richer the decoration on the upper section. The one at No. 14 *(photo at right)*, built in the first years of the 17th century, is outstanding. The house has what is known as a "step gable" and many windows with shutters all over the façade, as if the people who lived here wanted to enjoy the sunlight as much as possible, letting it flood into all the rooms. The rooms themselves were sober, the furnishings few, the floor uncovered: a simple place in all respects. The unusual and striking shape of the Sint Anthoniespoort (St. Antony's Gate) makes it recognizable from miles away. The gate, originally the eastern entrance to the city, is the only one extant from the Middle Ages. In 1617 it was turned into the Public Weighing Station, or Waag, and closed off by five massive towers. Although the groundfloor continued to be used as the weighing station until 1819, the upper floor became the headquarters of some of the local crafts guilds. Since 1975 the Waag has been occupied by the city's interest-ing Jewish Museum.

The Amstel is the river which crosses good part of the city and which gave the city its name. It was on the banks of the Amstel, as we have seen, that the first settlers founded what was to be the city of Amsterdam, and the names of the streets in this, the oldest part of the city, recall their origins. Running parallel to the Amstel on either side are two large canals, known collectively as the Voorburgwal, a name referring to the wall or moat in front of the city. The whole canal system linking Amsterdam is spanned by numerous bridges, but the Magere Brug (which means either Skinny Bridge or the

Interior of the Portuguese synagogue.

Anne Frank's house. ▶

bridge designed by Mager) is the most picturesque and is the only wooden drawbridge left on the Amstel. Ian Wagenaar, the city's historian, wrote that in his time (around the year 1765) there were no less than 250 bridges in Amsterdam, half of them made of wood. Originally built as a narrow foot-bridge, the Magere Brug was first enlarged and then had a movable section built into it in the center. Finally in 1772 it was converted into a double drawbridge. Standing on its slender arches, the bridge has an elegant appearance, but at night, when it is all lit up, it takes on an almost fairy-tale atmosphere.

The presence of the Jews in Holland and in particular in Amsterdam goes back to the second half of the 16th century. Most of them came here from Portugal. The long and bloody persecution of the Jews throughout the Iberian peninsula, especially in Spain, had caused their dispersion from the early 15th century on. Some of them had sought an escape by converting to Catholicism, but despite the fact that a few of the converts were notorious for their spiteful behaviour towards their brethren, most of these new Catholics, known as Marranos, had secretly kept alive their strong Jewish feeling. During

1481-1495, the Spanish Inquisition enacted still another bitter persecution against the Jews who found temporary refuge in Portugal. But in 1536 when the Inquisition was instituted in Portugal as well, the Marranos were forced to take flight once more. Luckily, Charles V granted them the right to settle in the Netherlands where, apart from a brief period of persecution instigated by the same Inquisition, they were able to benefit from the great tolerance following the Reformation and the success of the Union of Utrecht. The converts could thus rid themselves of their falsely-acquired Catholicism and return to the faith

The Vincent van Gogh Museum.

of their forefathers. Naturally, their origins were reflected in their houses of worship. This synagogue in Amsterdam is one of the most beautiful in the world; the vast building, the southeast façade of which faces toward Jerusalem, was erected between 1671 and 1675 by Elias Bouman and was restored in 1955. The **interior** consists of a single large hall, with three wooden barrel-vault ceilings, all the same size and held up by four Ionic columns.

The House of Anne Frank is at No. 263 Prinsengracht *(photo right)*. This young Jewish girl wrote the celebrated "Diary of Anne Frank" (called in Dutch "Het Achterhuis"), which was published in 1947. She hid in this house with her family and other Jews from July 8, 1942 to August 4, 1944, when their secret refuge was discovered and all the people in it arrested and deported. Anne Frank, taken to the concentration camp of Bergen-Belsen, died in March 1945, only two months before the liberation of Holland. The house today contains a thorough documentation of the deportation program carried out by the Germans against the Dutch and is visited by a continual stream of people who will not, cannot or feel they should never forget the significance of Anne Frank's story.

A huge zone on the left bank of the Singel, the outermost of the original circles surrounding the city contains the complex of Amsterdam's museums. Alongside the city's other great museum, the Stedelijk Museum, dedicated to the history and iconography of the city and of modern art, stands the modern building which the citizens of Amsterdam have dedicated to Van Gogh, the painter who committed suicide in 1890. The museum contains all the paintings and drawings which were exhibited in the Stedelijk while they were still the property of his heirs. The 95 canvases and 144 drawings were then left to the museum by a descendant of Van Gogh. This museum is also well-known as a center of activity in the art world.

Just beyond the Vincent Van Gogh Museum we find Holland's best-known art museum: the Rijksmuseum.

In 1808 the King of Holland, Louis Bonparte, placed on the throne by his brother, the Emperor Napoleon, decided to make Amsterdam not only the political but also the cultural capital of his kingdom. This was when the Town Hall on the Dam became the Royal Palace, and the king also created a royal art museum with its collections housed in several rooms of the palace's first floor. When Napoleon had the Kingdom of Holland incorporated into France, this became the Dutch Museum, which due to certain vicissitudes was never transferred elsewhere as planned. Then the new king, William I of the House of Orange, came to the throne, and he directed that the collections (which in the meantime had grown both in quantity and in quality) should remain in Amsterdam and that the museum should be called the Rijksmuseum van Schilderijen, or Museum of the Kingdom of the Netherlands. The works were later transferred to the Trippenhuis, an aristocratic dwelling built between 1660 and 1664 by the rich Trip brothers, where the museum was opened to the public in February 1817. It remained here for about seventy years, although space problems became more and more serious as the number of works it possessed continued to grow. In 1862 a competition was announced for the design of a new museum building, and 21 architects took part. Only ten years later the design submitted by P. J. H. Cuypers was accepted, and on 13 July 1885 the Rijksmuseum of Amsterdam, a grandiose building made from red brick in the neo-Gothic style, was officially opened. It has more than 260 rooms, containing not only masterpieces of painting but also superb prints, furniture, ceramics and other works of art. The major "attraction" of the museum is of course *Rembrandt Van Rijn's* **Night Watch.** This painting, one of his masterpieces and indeed a masterpiece of Western culture, was completed by the painter when he was 36 in 1642. The large canvas (measuring 4.38 by 3.59 meters, or about 14' × 10') was commissioned to celebrate the visit of Maria de' Medici to the city. Rembrandt painted the company of Captain Frans Cocq and his lieutenant Willem van Ruytenburch, a volunteer militia group, before the march. The name by which the

The Rijksmuseum.

The Nightwatch by Rembrandt.   *Rembrandt's House.*

painting is now universally known was given to it in the 18th century when, because of oxidation of the paint, the canvas came to acquire a "nocturnal" appearance. Rembrandt broke decisively with the then fashionable tradition of group portraits and placed the figures in his painting in dramatic poses.

Rembrandt, one of the greatest artists of all times, left a lasting imprint in the history of painting drawing, and engraving. Born in Leyden in 1606 to a bourgeois family, as a young man he enrolled in the local university to study humanities, but he soon left his studies and devoted himself exclusively to art. After training for several years in Leyden and Amsterdam, he decided to move to Amsterdam for good in 1631. His "Anatomy Lesson of Dr. Tulp" of 1632 brought him almost overnight fame. Contended as a portrait painter, he turned out a number of fine portraits during the period between 1636 and 1642, which was when his fame reached its highpoint. At the same time, however, his style was undergoing change and innovations were gradually being brought in. His brushwork grew broader and fuller and his palette, based on deep reds and browns with gold highlights, was becoming warmer and richer. The year 1642 was a turning point in Rembrandt's life. Deeply affected by deaths in his family, he started to change his style once more, whereupon he was able to attain an inner profundity which bestowed intensely dramatic and spiritual overtones to his painting. Throughout this period Rembrandt and his wife Saskia lived in a charming dwelling located on Sint Anthoniesbreestraat *(photo right)*. Turned into a museum in 1911, the house still preserves the atmosphere of when the master lived and worked in it. This period (1642-1655), although the least happy for Rembrandt from a personal standpoint, was his finest from an artistic one. From 1655 onwards, no longer understood and sought out by his contemporaries, he fell into great misery so that in 1656 he was forced to sell all his earthly possessions. He earned a living in partnership with his son Titus as a small-scale art dealer. The death of Titus in 1668 was the final blow dealt to this artist unique. Rembrandt died here in 1669.

The Castle of Muiden.

MUIDERSLOT

Muiderslot, which means castle of Muiden, is reached by crossing the river Vecht at its mouth on the Ijmeer where the tiny harbor of Muiden is located. On the site of the castle originally stood a wooden house which from the 10th century on served as a toll office for ships passing through. Founded in 1205 by the Bishop of Utrecht, the castle was enlarged again and again, especially under Count Floris V who in 1296 was murdered here. It was remodelled in the 15th century by Ludwig of Monfoort, During the 17th century, one of Holland's best loved poets, P. C. Hooft, lived in the castle. Today from the outside it looks like a sturdy brick cube with round towers at each corner. Inside there is a museum of history exhibiting tapestries, carpets, arms and armor, and furniture dating from the first half of the 17th century. One of the loveliest and most famous of these tapestries is the one depicting the encounter of Alexander the Great and the mother, wife, and daughters of Darius III after the battle of Isso, which was woven in Flanders in the 15th century.

UTRECHT

Situated on the banks of the Old Rhine (Oude Rijn), Utrecht was the religious capital of the Dutch Catholics for many centuries. Moreover, it is a great cultural center due to the presence of the world-famous University of Utrecht. The history of the city is crammed with events of great note. Long ago, at the beginning of the Christian era, the Rhine River flowed where the Cathedral of St. Martin now rises; nearby was a Roman encampment known as Albiobola. Because of its location by the river, the name of the settlement was changed from Trajectum ad Rhenum, i.e Rhine crossing, from which Utrajectum, then Trecht and finally the present-day Utrecht derived. The key year in the city's history is 696, for it was in that year that the Frankish kings and German emperors endowed Bishop St. Willibrord, apostle of the Frisians and the city's first bishop, with the land and power which would soon make Utrecht one of the most important religious centers of the Netherlands. Much later, in 1528, the Emperor Charles V annexed the territory to the Austrian-Hungarian empire and Utrecht, its power waning, was forced to give up its independent political status. In 1577 the citizens rose up against their Spanish conquerors, destroyed the symbol of Spanish power, the castle of Vreeburg, and drove the invaders from their homeland. Here two years later, on January 23, the United Provinces of the North signed the famous treaty known as the Union of Utrecht whereby they officially joined together against the Spanish domination. In 1580 in the throes of the Reformation, the last Catholic bishop departed from Utrecht and the city's religious supremacy started to decline; Utrecht would no longer be the spiritual center it had been up to then. By the same token, it was no longer the bustling business and trade center of the past, for, on one hand, the counts of Holland were progressively taking over more and more power and, on the other, cities such as Rotterdam, Amsterdam, and The Hague, more favorably situated on the coast, were growing increasingly

The University with the statue of J. van Nassau.

important as commercial centers. The history of Utrecht soon became lost in the mainstream of Dutch history, yet the city never fully let go of her supremacy over the other Dutch cities. In 1713 the peace treaty officially putting an end to the long bloody War of Spanish Succession was signed in Utrecht. And here too the Pontifical bull "Unigenitus" condemning Jansenism was emanated. The Bishop of Utrecht however refused to sign the document and the followers of John Huss flocked to the city which later became an asylum for the numerous Jansenists fleeing from nearby (Catholic) France. However, Utrecht's prestige and intellectual dominance were never really threatened by these events. The celebrated university founded in 1636 and the "School of Utrecht" founded by the painter Jan van Scorel in the 16th century contributed to the city's intellectual vigor. The school of Utrecht, for example, influenced by the Roman Mannerist painters, boasted outstanding arists such as Ter Brugghen, van Honthorst, and Poelemburgh among its ranks. The present-day university inside a building erected in 1883-1892 in the Flemish Renaissance style, incorporates what was originally the chapter hall of the former cathedral. The cathedral itself was built over an earlier building, the 7th century Cathedral of St. Martin, destroyed in a fire in 1253. A violent hurricane razed the whole nave to the ground in 1674 and all that was left standing was a long series of chapels and funerary monuments. In the vast Domplein these are separated from the Domtoren which has rightly been dubbed the "tower of the cathedral that is no longer there." The domtoren was built between 1321 and 1382 by Jan van Henegouwen, Godijn van Dormael, and Jan van den Doem. Rising 112 meters, it is the tallest in Holland — and also the loveliest, with its three levels, the first two square and the uppermost one octagonal, crowned by Flamboyant Gothic balconies.

The Domtoren.

The Koppelpoort.

AMERSFOORT

Founded in 777 and fortified at the beginning of the 12th century, Amersfoort experienced rapid and steady development even though the city never really benefited from Holland's golden age. The center of the city is a huge square called Onze-lieve-Vrouw Kerkhof, dominated by a lovely Gothic style belfry, the Toren. Soaring over 94 meters, it was originally built as the belltower for another church that was destroyed in 1787 when a gunpowder magazine unexpectedly blew up. It has been nicknamed Lange Jan (Long John) and is visible from far away. On top is a 30 bell carillon created by the famous bellfounders, the Hemonys. Particularly fascinating is the Koppelpoort, a fortified gate straddling the river Eem, which was put up in 1440 to control access to the town.

The Koornmarktspoort.

KAMPEN

Kampen enjoyed great prosperity throughout the Middle Ages (it belonged to the Hanseatic League) due to its favorable location at the mouth of the Ijssel. Then, with the progressive silting over of the river, and the closing off of the sea inside the city, like numerous other Dutch trading centers, Kampen began its decline. Three majestic city gates are all that is left of the city's glorious past: the Broderpoort, the Collenbroederspoort; and the Koornmarktspoort with its imposing round flanking towers.

DEVENTER

Set on the banks of the Ijssel, Deventer is perhaps best known to the tourist for its celebrated gingerbread, called Deventerkoek. Nonetheless, it should not be forgotten that throughout the Middle Ages and the Renaissance, the city was a lively cultural and religious center. Its vigorous intellectual life acted as a magnet for the philosophical, political, and religious greats of the times such as Erasmus, Pope Adrian VI, and Descartes (the latter resided in the city in 1632 and 1633). It was also a busy trading center; coins minted in Deventer have been discovered in several Baltic states and even as far as Russia. The history of Deventer is closely linked to the story of an Anglo-Saxon monk, Lebuinus, who came to the city in the 8th century in order to convert the local population. Lebuinus founded a tiny chapel on the spot where the Groote Kerk, or Sint Lebuinuskerk, rises today. In 1040 Bishop Bernold had a Romanesque basilica (stylistically related to the Renan sanctuaries) built on the spot, of which only the crypt is now extant. Despite the fact that the evident Gothic enlargements carried out in the 15th century considerably altered the original Romanesque structure of the basilica, it is still the most important momento of that period.

Sint Lebuinuskerk or Groote Kerk.

While the Groote Kerk is the city's major religious monument, the civic one of greatest luster is the Waag. The Waag, once a public weighing station and guardhouse, rises on the main square of the city, the Brink. It was built in the Gothic style in 1528 from the ruins of two fortifications, the Morgenster and the Altena, which originally stood on the opposite side of the river. These fortifications had been erected by the troops of the Duke of Gelderland, then furiously besieging the city. When the enemy was driven off, the inhabitants of Deventer destroyed the fortifications and triumphantly bore the remains back to their city. The building constructed from the ruins was a symbol of the renewed vigor of Deventer. Today the Waag and the Renaissance building adjoining it known as De drie gouden Haringen (the Three Golden Herrings) house the municipal museum collections. Another of the buildings on the Brink is the Penninckhuis, with its picturesque façade, dating from 1588. A typical example of a merchant's dwelling of the times, it is now partially a church and partially the European Center of the Albert Schweitzer Foundation.

◀ *The Waag.*

◀ *The Penninckshuis and statue of Albert Schweiter.*

ARNHEM

According to tradition, a part of the territory of Arnhem rises over the area which Tacitus had called Arenacum. But whatever the origins of the city may be, it evidently was soon considered an important cen- ter, since by the 13th century Otto III, Count of Gelderland, had grant- ed it the status of a city. Its highly favorable position on the right bank of the Neder Rijn (the Lower Rhine) was one of the major factors in stimulating rapid economic devel- opment. For almost two hundred years a member of the Hanseatic League, it was taken over by the Dukes of Burgundy when the Gelder dukes died out. It was actually the Emperor Charles V, heir to the Burgundy property, who did most to develop the city's great potential when he decided to set up the high court of justice in Arnhem. Phi- lip II followed suit when he estab- lished the administrative courts here. The city continued to prosper until, like all of the other Dutch cities, it was submerged by the fate-

The Stadhuis, popularly known as Duivelshuis.

ful events of the 17th and 18th centuries. In 1672 it fell to the French who left it two years later, only to reappear in 1799. Arnhem's name today evokes more recent, but even more tragic memories. In September 1944 an ill-fated landing attempted by a division of British parachutists provoked one of the fiercest battles fought in World War II. The city was destroyed and 7000 of the 10,000 British soldiers engaged in the battle were killed in action. One of the musts on a visit to Arnhem is the Stadhuis, popularly known as the Duivelshuis (the House of the Devil). Its incredible sculptural decoration makes it the most unusual sight in the city. Once the home of Maarten van Rossum, the famous general in the service of Charles of Gelderland, it was built between 1539 and 1546 in the Renaissance style. The corner projection leads to the lower floor where there is a portico sustained by three human figures with horsehoof feet. The façade is decorated with expertly carved human head and body sculptures. The Markt, a huge, modernday square, contains the city's principal buildings: an old city gate erected in 1357 and the Groote Kerk, or the Church of St. Eusebius, a basilica built in the 15th century in the late Gothic style with a lovely tower begun in 1452 by Arend van Gelder. Inside the building is the tomb of Charles of Gelder, a fine Renaissance style work of 1538.

◀ The Groote Kerk.

◀ The Sabelspoort.

Openluchtmuseum: windmills.

But one of the most fascinating sights in Arnhem — and one that is definitely unique in Holland — is the Openlucht Museum.

The full name of this unusual open-air museum is Rijksmuseum voor Volkskunde Nederlands Openlucht-Museum. It was founded in 1918 by a local historical society with quite an interesting idea in mind: several examples of Netherlandish rural architecture were either transported or reconstructed on 110 acres of park grounds. The visitor may thus follow the evolution of a

single style or the birth and development of a tradition. Each building is properly furnished and equipped with all that is required to carry out everyday activities. Thus, by following the route marked out for the sightseer, we can observe all the different kinds of homes from the various provinces: the hut with the straw roof from the Twente region dating from the 1600s (the oldest kind of Saxon rustic dwelling); the hut used by the fishermen of the Volendam area, so tiny it could only be used by a

single person at a time, from the north bank of the Ij; the watermill for the manufacture of paper; an oil plant from Zieuwent; a typical inn, the "De Hanekamp," from the Overijssel region. In the middle of the park there are five different types of windmill, each one built differently and thus used for a different purpose.

The ones shown here are of two different kinds; one is a sawmill dating from about 1700 and originally from Dordrecht, while the other was used to drain the polders

and was built in 1862 (its drainage capacity is 50-60 m³ of water per minute). Next to the two mills is a charming group of buildings which once formed the dwelling of a merchant from Koop (on the banks of the river `Zaan). The oldest part of the wooden house dates from 1686. Later, other wings were added to the core and the building gradually became what we see to-day. The interior is in perfect keeping with the bourgeois style that dominated the 19th century.

Rather different in style and taste is this rustic farm building from Midlum in Friesland, typical of the region throughout the 17th century. The most interesting parts are the granary, an immense aisled structure rebuilt in 1778, and the kitchen which is completely furnished with period pieces.

Openluchtmuseum: merchants' houses.

Openluchtmuseum:
interior of a farmhouse from Midlum.

During the second half of the 15th century, the invention of printing led to an increase in the consumption and demand for paper, whereby creating a boom in the paper industry. The technique of using a mill as a power source for the whole range of human activities could hardly be ignored in the development of paper-making. One of the Openluchtmuseum's most fascinating historical relics is a watermill originally part of a tiny papermill in Veluwe in Gelderland, dating from the mid 1800s. From it, we can get an idea of how paper was made a hundred years ago. The power produced by water falling from the mill wheel was used to finely grind linen rags inside a kind of giant mortar equipped with hammers as well as to run the "Dutchman" (a machine with revolving blades in which the resulting linen pulp underwent further mashing). This pulp was then manually drained on wooden frames and a metal strainer until the fibers sedimented and a sheet of paper was obtained. The raw paper was placed between two felt pads and pressed to make the fibers better stick together and then dried out.

Openluchtmuseum; paper mill: the "Dutchman".

Openluchtmuseum; paper mill: producing the sheets.

Openluchtmuseum; paper mill: pressing the sheets between felt pads.

NIJMEGEN

Nijmegen, nestling on the hills of the left bank of the river Waal, rises on the site of a Batavian "oppidum" which was destroyed in 69 A.D. by the Roman legions who had come to quell a revolt. The Romans then founded a settlement called Noviomagus on the spot which in 105 A.D. Trajan proclaimed a Roman city with the name of Ulpia Noviomagus. Set on a plain overlooking the river is the Valkhof, literally "falcon park" since Charlemagne's son, Louis the Pious, used to raise hunting falcons here. Here too in 768 Charlemagne had a palace built for himself which soon became one of his favorite residences. Sacked numerous times by the Normans, it was rebuilt by Frederick the Redbeard in 1152. Today all that is left of the old building, witness to so many historical events, is an octagonal brick baptistry consecrated by Leo III in 799. Despite the addition of a Gothic apse, the name Carolingian Chapel has remained to this day.

The Waag.

The Carolingian Chapel.

The Kröller-Müller Museum.

HOGE VELUWE

Despite the fact that Veluwe actually means "sterile land" in Dutch, the Hoge Veluwe National Park, extending over almost 15,000 acres, is filled with peaceful woods, moors, and meadows of great beauty. Deer, mouflon, and other wildlife are completely free to roam the park. The park also contains the Rijksmuseum Kröller-Müller, one of the most important of the Dutch art museums, founded by Helene Kröller-Müller, wife of a famous Dutch businessman. The architect Ludwig Mies van der Rohe was asked to submit a design, but it was rejected and the project was then awarded to Henri van de Velde who began work on it in 1863, For the celebration of the first centennial of Van Gogh's birth in 1953 another wing was added on and the building could thus finally be considered finished. On display inside are paintings from all Dutch schools from the 15th century onwards; but the museum's greatest treasure is its collection of modern paintings, especially those by Van Gogh. There are over 300 Van Goghs displayed in the museum, which makes it the biggest Van Gogh collection in the world. Back in the park, do not overlook a visit to the Sint Hubertus which is a hunting lodge built in 1926 by Berlage in the form of deer horns.

's HERTOGENBOSCH

Known also as Den Bosch, this historical city of Brabant of the North is famous as the birthplace of one of the world's greatest painters: Hieronymus Aken, called Bosch, who was born here in 1450 and died here in 1516. The Duke of Brabant, Henry I, granted municipal rights to the city in 1185. This marked the beginning of a long period of prosperity which extended throughout the 14th and 15th centuries. But the three sieges that 's Hertogenbosch was put to are just as famous. The first one took place in 1601, when Maurice, Prince of Orange, besieged it for 27 days, the second in 1603, and the third, which lasted five months, was begun by Prince Frederick Henry in 1629. The whole town is dominated by the imposing bulk of the Cathedral of St. John, the Sint Janskathedraal, the loveliest Dutch church in the Brabant Flamboyant style. Built between 1419 and 1530, it rises on the site of a former Romanesque basilica burnt down in a fire. Numerous artists contributed to the building of the cathedral, among whom were Jan Heyns and Alart du Hameel. The outside is a flurry of gargoyles, pinnacles, and picturesque details such as figurines, statuettes, and drôleries placed astride the buttresses, perched upon the pinnacles, and sticking to the gargoyles. The chiaroscuro effect of the decorative elements joined to the volumetric effect of the masses lightens the whole and creates an incredible plastic tension. Likewise, the inside is truly effective: the double aisles are divided by 150 columns without capitals, each one decorated by a 16th century statue. There are several noteworthy pieces to be enjoyed, such as the 4 meter tall copper baptismal font executed by Aert de Maastricht, the carved pulpit from the mid 1600s, and, at the end of the left aisle, a wooden statue of the Virgin of the 13th century.

The Cathedral of Sint Jans. ▶

Detail of the decoration of Sint Jans. ▶

MAASTRICHT

Situated on the banks of the Maas, capital of Dutch Limburg, Maastricht is strangely wedged in between Holland, Germany, and Belgium. In fact, as the convergence point of three so very different civilizations, it has a curious mixture of three languages, life styles, and monetery systems. When in 1830 Belgium broke off from the realm, Maastricht did not take part in the secessionist movement and thus the province to which it continued to belong, Limburg, penetrates like a wedge into the territory of West Germany (in fact, Aquisgrana can be reached by bus in just 20 minutes). During the Roman era, Maastricht, due to its position as a river crossing, was known as Trajectum ad Mosam. Here the Romans had set up a military encampment which later became a settlement. In 382 St. Servatius arrived and established a bishopric here which in 722 was moved to Liege by Charlemagne, whereby provoking a longstanding rivalry between the bishops of Liege and the dukes of Brabant. After the death of St. Servatius in 384, a basilica founded by the bishops Monulfus and Gundulfus was built over the site of his tomb. Thus, the city actually consisted of two urban centers: the earlier one which had grown up by the Maas and the later one which had grown up around the monastery. The two parishes were joined up in 1229 but this did not lead to political union — in fact, the split continued all the way up to 1794. Maastricht soon found economic prosperity in the cloth trade, especially in the 12th and 13th centuries, but in the 15th and 16th centuries its fortune began to decline when it was subjected to numerous sieges. Alessandro Farnese, Duke of Parma, was responsible for the cruelest, that of 1579, but no less famous is the one conducted by Louis XIV in 1673. One of the French soldiers engaged in battle was Captian d'Artagnan, the legendary musketeer immortalized by Alexander Dumas in his novel "The Three Musketeers," who met his death during the siege. The damage that the population of Maastricht had suffered during the wars

Sint Servaas and Sint Janskerk viewed from the Vrijhof.

The Sint Janskerk.

The Stadhuis.

The Helpoort.

of the past centuries were fortunately spared her during the Second World War as the population found refuge in the maze of underground tunnels inside the mountain named after St. Peter to the south of the city. The major center of attraction, in addition to the Baroque Stadhuis designed by Pieter Post and the 13th century Helpoort (Hell's Gate), is the Vrijthof, or weapon court, on which there are two churches, namely Sint Servaaskerk and Sint Janskerk. Sint Servaaskerk, built in the Mosan Romanesque style, is the oldest church in Holland. It was founded about 570 by the bishops Monulfus and Gundulfus, destroyed by the Normans in 831, and then rebuilt around 950. The apse is especially noteworthy. In pure end of the 12th century Romanesque style, it is flanked by square towers and surmounted by a delicate gallery. On the west side of the church is a majestic Mosan style porch — this is the oldest surviving part of the building. The porch comprises three storeys of blind arches in the Lombard style, supported by arched buttresses which, quaintly enough, serve as a road underpass. Beside it is Sint Janskerk, in the Gothic style of the mid 1500s, which after 1632 was reconsecrated to the Protestant cult. Another masterpiece of Mosan Romanesque art in Maastricht is the church of Onze Lieve Vrouwekerk, the oldest sanctuary in the city. Founded in 380 on the site of a pagan temple, it consists of a high wall flanked by slender cylindrical towers pierced only by a few narrow openings which add to its imposing regal appearance. The unusual composition of the façade and the squat, impressive looking apse make it somewhat resemble the Cathedral of Worms.

◀ *Vroumekerk.*

The Groote Kerk of Breda. ▶

BREDA

The quiet life in present-day Breda, a modern industrial center situated at the confluence of the Mark and Aa rivers, is quite a contrast to the battles and fights which it was witness to in the past. The painting by Velazquez which immortaliz-ed the surrender of the city to the Marquis of Spinola in 1625 after nine months of siege is well-known to everyone. The Groote Kerk, erected between 1468 and 1509, is an example of the Brabantine Gothic style of the end of the 15th-early 16th centuries.

MIDDELBURG

Capital of the province of Zeeland, a region which for centuries was contended by the sea, the city is situated on the Isle of Walcheren and connected to the mainland. Middelburg's development had its start about 1100 around an abbey of Premonstratensian monks. The flourishing cloth trade carried on with England and the lucrative importation of French wine made Middelburg so prosperous throughout the Middle Ages that it even rivaled Bruges. In the 17th and 18th centuries the East India Company set up a great warehouse in the city and this increased its prosperity even more. In all its long history, Middelburg suffered the greatest damage when, during World War II, on May 17, 1940, fire bombs dropped by the German air force rained upon the city's major monuments, thus causing death and destruction. Nevertheless, thanks to the loving care of those who desired that they be repaired and restored, the monuments were brought back to life and today they can be enjoyed in all their splendor.

On the Middelburg Markt stands what is considered the most beautiful and what is definitely the most elaborately adorned Stadhuis in Holland. The façade is typically Flemish, a masterpice of the Flamboyant Gothic style. On the first level are statues depicting the counts of Zeeland and their wives. They are placed inside double niches between the windows and surmounted by finely-carved little canopies. Another unusual feature of the

Aerial view of Middelburg with its picturesque star-shaped canal system.

The Stadhuis. ▶

building is the 55 meter tall belfry with four little towers at each corner which are joined to the central one by delicate little buttresses. Middelburg's most precious jewel, however, is the huge and grandiose Abbey which is reached by way of a tiny square known as Balans. The complex, today the headquarters for the province's government offices, was founded in about 1100 and was occupied by the monastic order of the Premonstratensians from 1128 to 1559. The abbey actually comprises two churches, i.e. the Nieuwe Kerk and the Koorkerk. The former, in the Flamboyant Gothic style, has no aisles and is noteworthy for its unusual star-shaped stone vaulting. The latter, 14th century Gothic in style, houses the Nicolai organ built in Utrecht between 1479 and 1481. Between the two churches is the 87 meter high tower known as Lange Jan (Long John); although it was erected between the 14th and 15th centuries, it is surmounted by an 18th century cusp. Just beyond the abbey is the Oudhospitaal, an old military hospital in the Flemish Renaissance style of the 17th century. It has an unusual high sloping roof with painted dormers. Above the central portal of the façade is an imperial eagle with outspread wings.

The most impressive view of the city however is afforded by an aerial panorama which shows its striking plan, surely the most unusual in all of Holland. The historic center, enclosed within a circular roadway, is surrounded by a double band of star-shaped canals. The plan has been attributed to van Coehoorn, general consultant for the fortifications of the United Provinces in the 17th century and military engineer of the school of Vanban.

◀ *The Oudehospitaal.*

◀ *The Nieuwe Kerk with the "Lange Jan" tower.*

The inner courtyard of the abbey.

VEERE

Even though it was never really totally abandoned, Veere is considered one of the many "dead cities" of the Netherlands. Its prosperity came about when Wolfaert van Borselen of Veere married Mary Stuart, the daughter of James I, and thus became a member of the Scottish royal family. As a result, the van Borselens obtained the exclusive right to import raw wool from Scotland which they sent off to the Bruges cloth merchants who made magnificent cloth out of it. The merchants of Veere soon became very wealthy. Proof of this flourishing commerce with the Scots are the Schotse Huisen (Scots' Houses) along the shore. These were erected in the 16th century in the Flamboyant Gothic style to house the Scottish traders when they came to Veere to sell their wool. More than anyone else, of course, it was the van Borselen family that benefited from all of this commercial activity. In 1474 they had the Stadhuis built and the façade decorated with seven statues of members of their family with their respective wives. The city's importance began to wane in the 16th century due to the war of independence Holland was then waging against Spain and the closing off of the sea which brought an end to trade with Scotland. Coming from afar, the visitor is immediately struck by the appearance of the Groote Kerk, in the late Gothic style, which was built by Anthonis and Rombout Keldermans in the 14th century. In 1811 during the French occupation, Napoleon had it transformed into a hospital and, in order to keep out the icy north winds, he had the tomb slabs removed from the flooring and put over the windows. And this is just how we see it today.

◀ *Panorama.*
◀ *The Stadhuis.*

The Schotse Huizen.

Oosterscheldebrug.

OOSTERSCHELDEBRUG

Throughout the centuries long fight that the Dutch people have been waging against the sea, the problem of Zeeland has always been one of the most burning issues — the very name Zeeland means the "the sea's land" in Dutch. After the disastrous flood which took place on St. Elizabeth's Day in 1421, the Dutch were convinced that they would never again go through such a terrible experience. But they were wrong, for five centuries later, on February 1, 1953, disaster struck once more when a violent hurricane coming from northwest encountered a high tide which was then rising. The dikes, hit from both sides, gave way and the sea flooded all of Zeeland and north Brabant, devasting even the southernmost zones of the country. Yet the Dutch, evidently accustomed to such disasters by their long history of natural calamities, once more rose to the occasion, and in a few short months were able to re-organize life in the devasted areas. Thereafter, they decided to carry out a huge undertaking, dubbed the Delta Project, which entailed closing all the sea tongues to be found between the estuary of the Schelda and the canal of Rotterdam. Part of this bold project is the Oosterscheldebrug, inaugurated in 1966, whose 5,022 meter length makes it the longest bridge in Europe. Its 52 spans rest upon poured concrete pylons which in some cases have been sunk 30 meters into the water.

INDEX